My Practice Workbook

with Kids Club

Times Tables

Ages 5-7

This book belongs to: ....

Fill in your certificate when you have completed this book.

I completed this book on

Date: ....

Signature: ....

Well done

HODDER Education

Advice for parents and carers

This book focuses on numbers from 1 to 10. Although children can complete the activities on their own, you may like to work with them for the first few pages.

- Don't get your child to do too much at once. A 'little and often' approach is a good start.

- Reward your child with lots of praise and encouragement.

- Talk to your child about what they have learnt and what they can do.

- The '**Get ready**' section provides a gentle warm-up for the topic covered on the page.

- The '**Let's practise**' section consolidates understanding of the topic. The questions in this section get progressively harder.

- The '**Have a go**' section is often a challenge or something interesting that your child can go away and do. It may require your child to use everyday objects around the house.

- The '**How have I done?**' section is a short informal test that should be attempted when all the units have been completed. It is useful for spotting any gaps in knowledge, which can then be revisited at a suitable moment.

- The '**Tips from teachers**' give useful advice on specific topics or skills, to deepen your child's understanding and confidence and to help you help your child.

Times Tables

This book reinforces the conceptual understanding of multiplying and dividing and practises the multiplication and division facts that your child will need to know between the ages of 5 and 7 years. Give your child opportunities to count backwards and forwards in different steps and encourage them to see multiplication as repeated addition and division as the repeated subtraction of groups. Practise the ×2, ×5 and ×10 tables facts each week, moving on to the ×3 and ×4 tables when appropriate.

By age 7, most children should be able to:

- understand that halving is the opposite of doubling and recall doubles of all numbers to 20 and the corresponding halves

- recall multiplication and division facts for the 2, 5 and 10 multiplication tables

- use the multiplication (×), division (÷) and equals (=) signs to read and write mathematical statements

- recognise and use the inverse relationship between multiplication and division to check calculations

- recognise and show that multiplication can be done in any order and division cannot

- solve word problems involving multiplication and division.

Hachette UK's policy is to use papers that are natural, renewable and recyclable products and made from wood grown in well-managed forests and other controlled sources. The logging and manufacturing processes are expected to conform to the environmental regulations of the country of origin.

Orders: please contact Hachette UK Distribution, Hely Hutchinson Centre, Milton Road, Didcot, Oxfordshire, OX11 7HH. Telephone: +44 (0)1235 827827. Email education@hachette.co.uk Lines are open from 9 a.m. to 5 p.m., Monday to Friday. You can also order through our website: www.hoddereducation.co.uk

ISBN: 9781398388857

© Paul Broadbent & Peter Patilla 2023

First published in 2013. This edition published in 2023 by Hodder Education, an Hachette UK Company, Carmelite House, 50 Victoria Embankment, London EC4Y 0DZ

MIX
Paper | Supporting responsible forestry
FSC™ C104740
www.fsc.org

Typeset and printed in the UK. Character illustrations by Lisa Hunt from the Bright Agency. Other illustrations by Chantelle and Burgen Thorne, and Fakenham Prepress Solutions. A catalogue record for this title is available from the British Library.

Impression number 10 9 8 7 6 5 4 3 2 1

Year 2027 2026 2025 2024 2023

Contents

Colour the stars as you go!

Welcome to Kids Club!

Hi, readers. My name's Charlie and I run Kids Club with my friend Abbie. Kids Club is an after-school club that is very similar to one somewhere near you.

We'd love you to come and join our club and see what we get up to!

I'm Abbie and I run Kids Club with Charlie. Let's meet the kids who will work with you on the activities in this book.

My name's Jamelia. I look forward to Kids Club every day. The sports and games are my favourites, especially on Kids Camp in the school holidays.

Hi, I'm Megan. I've made friends with all the children at Kids Club. I like the outings and trips we go on the best.

Hello, my name's Jae. Kids Club is a great place to chill out after school. My best friend is Alfie – everyone knows Alfie!

I'm Amina. I like to do my homework at Kids Club. Charlie and Abbie are always very helpful. We're like one big happy family.

Greetings, readers. My name's Alfie! Everybody knows me here. Come and join our club. We'll have a great time together!

Now you've met us all, tell us something about yourself. All the kids filled in a '**Personal profile**' when they joined.

Here's one for you to complete.

DRAW A PICTURE OF YOURSELF HERE

Name: _____

Age: _____

School: _____

Home town: _____

Pets: _____

My favourite:

✳ book is _____,

✳ film is _____,

✳ food is _____,

✳ sport is _____.

My hero is _____ because _____

_____.

When I grow up I want to be a _____.

If I could be king or queen for the day, the first thing I would do is _____

_____.

If I could be any animal for a day I would be a _____

_____.

Grouping

I'm helping Abbie sort a cupboard. We need to count things before we put them back. I'm going to group objects, then count the groups. This is a useful way of counting large numbers. Can you help me?

I have put these balloons in groups of 3.
There are 5 groups.
5 groups of 3 balloons make 15 balloons altogether.

Get ready

Count these groups.

1. [ ] groups of 3 make [ ].

2. [ ] groups of 5 make [ ].

3. [ ] groups of 10 make [ ].

4. [ ] groups of 2 make [ ].

5. [ ] groups of 4 make [ ].

6. [ ] groups of 5 make [ ].

Tips from teachers

Making and counting groups is a step towards repeated addition which is a useful model for multiplication. Make sure your child understands that the objects need to be in equal groups before counting each group.

Colour the star when you complete the page.

Can you group these objects for me? Draw a circle round each group. Then count how many groups and how many altogether.

7 [ ] groups of 3 make [ ].

8 [ ] groups of 2 make [ ].

9 [ ] groups of 4 make [ ].

10 [ ] groups of 3 make [ ].

11 [ ] groups of 5 make [ ].

Have a go

Group these balloons and count them.

12 By colour: [ ] groups of [ ]   14 By size: [ ] groups of [ ]

13 By shape: [ ] groups of [ ]   15 How many balloons are there altogether? [ ]

7

Repeated addition

We went on a trip to the seaside with Kids Club. Count these shells in groups of two.

$$2 + 2 + 2 + 2 = 8$$
2 repeated 4 times = 8

⭐ **Get ready**

Count these groups and write the answers.

1 3   +   3   +   3   = ☐

2 2 + 2 + 2 + 2 + 2 + 2   = ☐

3 5   +   5   +   5   = ☐

4 4   +   4   = ☐

5 5 + 5 + 5 + 5   = ☐

6 3 + 3 + 3 + 3 + 3 + 3 + 3   = ☐

7 2 + 2 + 2 + 2   = ☐

8 4   +   4   +   4   +   4   +   4   = ☐

Tips from teachers

Repeated addition is one of the models used to represent multiplication at this stage. The relationship between the two concepts is often an area of difficulty. 2 + 2 + 2 + 2 is 2 repeated 4 times, which is 2 multiplied by 4 or 2 × 4. We address the fact that the × sign does not directly relate to the term 'groups of' on pages 12–13.

Colour the star when you complete the page.

Count these groups and write the answers.

9

5 repeated 2 times is ☐.

10

3 repeated 5 times is ☐.

11

4 repeated 7 times is ☐.

12

10 repeated 3 times is ☐.

13

2 repeated 2 times is ☐.

Have a go

Count the wheels in each row.

14

2 wheels repeated 8 times = ☐ wheels.

15

4 wheels repeated 4 times = ☐ wheels.

16

3 wheels repeated 6 times = ☐ wheels.

17

10 wheels repeated 2 times = ☐ wheels.

Colour the star when you complete the page.

Multiplying

I've collected beans from the Kids Club garden – but I prefer beans from a can! Look at how I've grouped these to help me multiply.

$$5 + 5 + 5 = 15$$
$$5 \text{ multiplied by } 3 = 15$$
$$5 \times 3 = 15$$

Get ready

Count the groups and complete the multiplication.

1

2 multiplied by 5 = ☐

2

3 multiplied by 2 = ☐

3

10 multiplied by 4 = ☐

4

5 multiplied by 6 = ☐

5

4 multiplied by 4 = ☐

6

2 multiplied by 9 = ☐

Tips from teachers

Emphasise that the multiplication sign means 'multiplied by', so the first number in the calculation is 'operated on' by the second number. This relates to repeated addition so that the first number is the number in each group and the second number shows how many groups there are. So with this model, 4 × 3 is represented by 4 + 4 + 4 and not by 3 + 3 + 3 + 3.

Colour the star when you complete the page.

 **Let's practise**

Answer these.

7 $4 + 4 + 4 + 4 + 4 =$ ☐

$4 \times 5 =$ ☐

8 $5 + 5 =$ ☐

$5 \times 2 =$ ☐

9 $3 + 3 + 3 + 3 + 3 + 3 + 3 + 3 + 3 + 3 =$ ☐

$3 \times 10 =$ ☐

10 $2 + 2 + 2 + 2 + 2 + 2 + 2 =$ ☐

$2 \times 7 =$ ☐

11 $3 + 3 + 3 =$ ☐

$3 \times 3 =$ ☐

12 $10 + 10 + 10 + 10 =$ ☐

$10 \times 4 =$ ☐

Have a go

13 Write the numbers coming out of this multiplication machine.

1		
2		
3		
4		
5	in →	out →
6		
7		
8		
9		
10		

X 2

11

Arrays

I like sewing and if I put these buttons on the side of my bag in this pattern it will help me multiply.

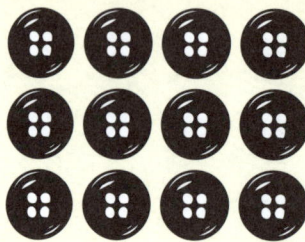

Look at these buttons.

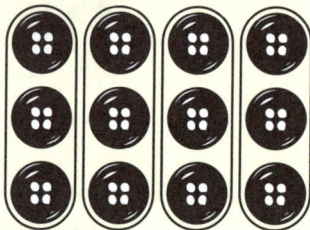
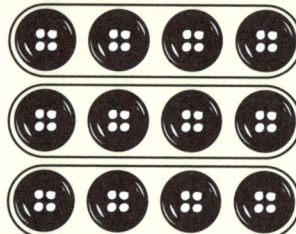

The buttons can be counted in 3s.
3 + 3 + 3 + 3 = 12
3 multiplied by 4 = 12
3 × 4 = 12

The buttons can be counted in 4s.
4 + 4 + 4 = 12
4 multiplied by 3 = 12
4 × 3 = 12

3 × 4 has the same answer as 4 × 3.

Get ready

Complete these multiplications.

1
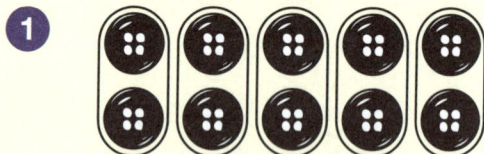

2 × ☐ = ☐

3

3 × ☐ = ☐

2

10 × ☐ = ☐

4
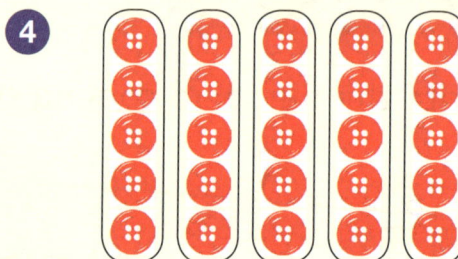

5 × ☐ = ☐

Tips from teachers

Arranging objects into a rectangular array helps to reinforce that multiplication is commutative. This means the order doesn't affect the outcome (3 × 4 = 4 × 3). Arrays can be arranged vertically or horizontally, but the way they are grouped links the repeated addition to the multiplication, i.e. 3 + 3 + 3 + 3 is linked to 3 × 4. Addition is also commutative (4 + 6 = 6 + 4), but subtraction and division are not.

Colour the star when you complete the page.

Write a multiplication to match each array.

5

☐ × ☐ = ☐

6

☐ × ☐ = ☐

7

☐ × ☐ = ☐

8
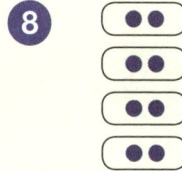

☐ × ☐ = ☐

9
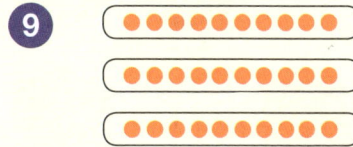

☐ × ☐ = ☐

10
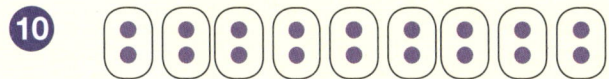

☐ × ☐ = ☐

Have a go

Write two multiplications for each array.

11

☐ × ☐ = ☐

☐ × ☐ = ☐

12

☐ × ☐ = ☐

☐ × ☐ = ☐

13

☐ × ☐ = ☐

☐ × ☐ = ☐

What do you notice?

13

Doubling and halving

Jae was really good today so I said he could have double his time on the computer. Jae didn't know that doubling was getting the same amount again! I used the cubes to explain doubling. Look at these patterns.

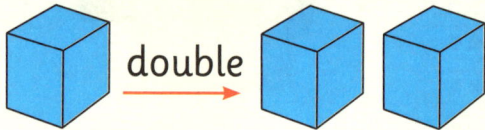

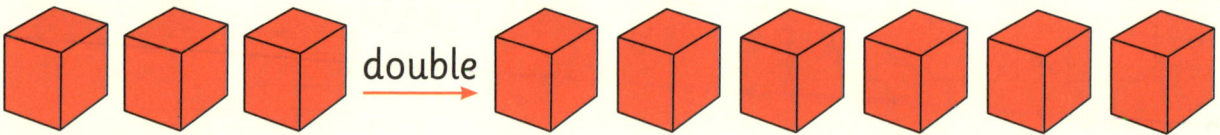

⭐ Get ready

Draw double these spots and write how many.

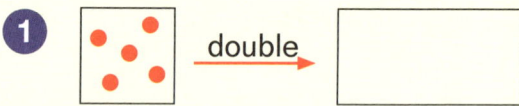

5 → ☐

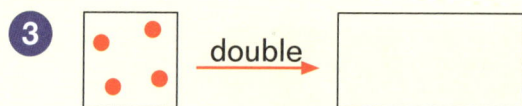

4 → ☐

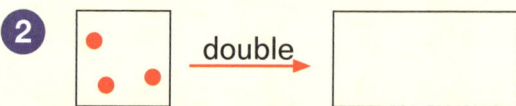

3 → ☐

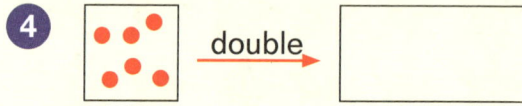

6 → ☐

Tips from teachers

Being able to double and halve numbers quickly and accurately is a useful skill to support mental calculations. For example, when adding 6 and 7 it is a good strategy to double 6 and then add 1. Help your child to practise doubling numbers to 20 and multiples of 10 and then relate this to halving.

Colour the star when you complete the page.

Alfie was not good today so I said he would only have half his time on the computer. I used the cubes to explain halving.

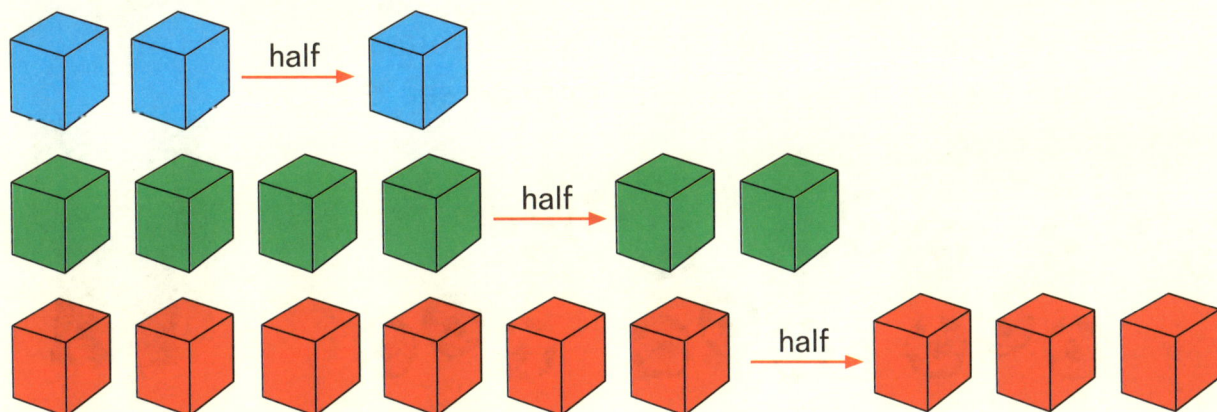

Let's practise

5 Write the numbers coming out of this halving machine.

in		out
2		
4		
6		
8		
10		
12		

Have a go

Doubling is the same as × 2. Halving is the same as ÷ 2.

6 Join each of these to the matching answer.

16 ÷ 2   12 ÷ 2   3 × 2   40 ÷ 2

8 × 2   9 × 2   6 × 2   10 × 2

20 ÷ 2   7 × 2

6
8
10
12
14
16
18
20

15

Colour the star when you complete the page.

Dividing

I'm in charge of sports clubs this week and each team needs 3 balls.

There are 18 balls and I have taken away groups of 3 until there are no more balls left. You can see the groups of 3 here.

How many groups of 3 are there in 18?
There are 6 groups of 3.

Charlie explained that 18 put into groups of 3 is the same as 18 divided by 3. So, 18 divided by 3 is 6.

Get ready

Complete these divisions.

1. 16 divided by 2 is ☐.

2. 24 divided by 3 is ☐.

3. 28 divided by 4 is ☐.

4. 30 divided by 5 is ☐.

Tips from teachers

Use grouping rather than sharing as a model for division, as this will help your child when dividing large numbers. For example, for 15 divided by 3, group 15 into 3s and use repeated subtraction of those groups until you reach zero. Count the groups to show, for example, that 15 divided by 3 is 5. This relates to how many groups of 3 there are in 15.

Let's practise

Put the objects into groups and complete the divisions.

5

`2 x BATS`

[ ] grouped into 2 = [ ] groups
[ ] divided by 2 = [ ]

6

`5 x shirts`

[ ] grouped into 5 = [ ] groups
[ ] divided by 5 = [ ]

7

`4 x whistles`

[ ] grouped into 4 = [ ] groups
[ ] divided by 4 = [ ]

8

`3 goggles`

[ ] grouped into 3 = [ ] groups
[ ] divided by 3 = [ ]

9

`5 x balls`

[ ] grouped into 5 = [ ] groups
[ ] divided by 5 = [ ]

10

`3 x medals`

[ ] grouped into 3 = [ ] groups
[ ] divided by 3 = [ ]

Have a go

Count in jumps of 2s, 3s, 4s, and 6s on this number line.

1	2	3	4	5	6	7	8	9	10	11	12	13	14	15	16	17	18	19	20	21	22	23	24

11 How many 2s in 24? [ ]   **13** How many 4s in 24? [ ]

12 How many 3s in 24? [ ]   **14** How many 6s in 24? [ ]

Colour the star when you complete the page.

17

Multiplying by 2, 5 and 10

I like patterns and these multiplication patterns are really interesting. Starting at zero the pink line counts in 2s, the blue line counts in 5s and the numbers in the 10s count are shaded.
Can you find 5 × 3 on the number line?

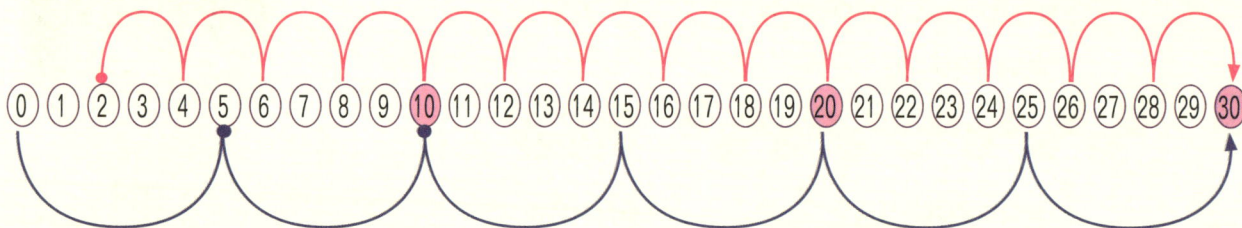

0 1 2 3 4 5 6 7 8 9 10 11 12 13 14 15 16 17 18 19 20 21 22 23 24 25 26 27 28 29 30

Get ready

Continue each pattern.

1 Count in 2s and shade the number.

2 Count in 10s and circle each number.

3 Count in 5s and cross each number.

1	2	3	4	5	6	7	8	9	10
11	12	13	14	15	16	17	18	19	20
21	22	23	24	25	26	27	28	29	30
31	32	33	34	35	36	37	38	39	40

Tips from teachers

Encourage your child to look at the pattern of the results when multiplying a number by 2, 5 and 10, showing that × 10 is double × 5 and saying them in order to begin with so that they learn the order. Eventually they should know each multiplication fact by heart out of order, so start identifying the ones they know and those they are yet to learn.

Colour the star when you complete the page.

4 Answer these and try to learn them.

2 × 1 = ☐
2 × 2 = ☐
2 × 3 = ☐
2 × 4 = ☐
2 × 5 = ☐
2 × 6 = ☐
2 × 7 = ☐
2 × 8 = ☐
2 × 9 = ☐
2 × 10 = ☐
2 × 11 = ☐
2 × 12 = ☐

5 × 1 = ☐
5 × 2 = ☐
5 × 3 = ☐
5 × 4 = ☐
5 × 5 = ☐
5 × 6 = ☐
5 × 7 = ☐
5 × 8 = ☐
5 × 9 = ☐
5 × 10 = ☐
5 × 11 = ☐
5 × 12 = ☐

10 × 1 = ☐
10 × 2 = ☐
10 × 3 = ☐
10 × 4 = ☐
10 × 5 = ☐
10 × 6 = ☐
10 × 7 = ☐
10 × 8 = ☐
10 × 9 = ☐
10 × 10 = ☐
10 × 11 = ☐
10 × 12 = ☐

Have a go

5 Join these multiplications to their answers.

2 × 10   5 × 4   10 × 3

2 × 9   5 × 5   10 × 4

| 10 |
| 12 |
| 15 |
| 18 |
| 20 |
| 25 |
| 30 |
| 40 |
| 45 |
| 50 |

5 × 6   5 × 8

5 × 9

5 × 3   10 ×1   5 × 10

5 × 2

2 × 6

Colour the star when you complete the page.

Multiplying by 1 and 0

I'm helping Jae with the sports this week. These balls are kept in boxes. I have one full box and one empty box. If you multiply any number by 1, the number stays the same.

1 group of 5 makes 5.
$5 \times 1 = 5$ and $1 \times 5 = 5$

If you multiply any number by 0, the answer is 0.

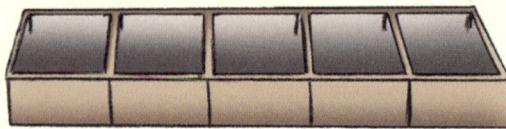

0 groups of 5 make 0.
$5 \times 0 = 0$ and $0 \times 5 = 0$

Get ready

Write two multiplications for each of these.

1 ☐ × ☐ = 6
☐ × ☐ = 6

2 ☐ × ☐ = 0
☐ × ☐ = 0

3 ☐ × ☐ = 4
☐ × ☐ = 4

4 ☐ × ☐ = 0
☐ × ☐ = 0

5 ☐ × ☐ = 9
☐ × ☐ = 9

6 ☐ × ☐ = 0
☐ × ☐ = 0

Colour the star when you complete the page.

Let's practise

7 Draw a circle around the multiplications with an answer of zero. Then join the remaining multiplications to their matching answer.

1 1×3

4 1×9

7 0×8

0×7 0×2

8 6×0

5×0 3×0

3   **6** 2×1

8×1 9×0 6×1

2 1×7 **5** 5×1 4×0 **9**

0×1

Have a go

Write the missing numbers.

8 $8 \times 1 = \boxed{}$

9 $6 \times 0 = \boxed{}$

10 $0 \times 9 = \boxed{}$

11 $1 \times 4 = \boxed{}$

12 $\boxed{} \times 1 = 6$

13 $7 \times \boxed{} = 0$

14 $\boxed{} \times 4 = 0$

15 $1 \times \boxed{} = 9$

Tips from teachers

Multiplying any number by one is an easier concept to understand than multiplying by zero, as it can be modelled practically with 'one group of . . .' To help understand, for example, 5×0, use 'no groups of 5' as a model. Reinforce the idea with the pattern of repeated subtraction: $5 \times 3 = \mathbf{15}$, $5 \times 2 = \mathbf{10}$, $5 \times 1 = \mathbf{5}$, $5 \times 0 = \mathbf{0}$.

Colour the star when you complete the page.

Multiplying by 3

I've planted flowers in rows of 3 – my favourite number!
It helps me practise multiplying by 3.
Here are 8 rows of 3 plants.

$3 \times 8 = 24$
$8 \times 3 = 24$

Get ready

Practise multiplying by 3. Answer these questions.

1

$3 \times 2 = \boxed{}$
$2 \times 3 = \boxed{}$

2

$3 \times 5 = \boxed{}$
$5 \times 3 = \boxed{}$

3

$3 \times 10 = \boxed{}$
$10 \times 3 = \boxed{}$

4

$3 \times 7 = \boxed{}$
$7 \times 3 = \boxed{}$

5

$3 \times 6 = \boxed{}$
$6 \times 3 = \boxed{}$

6

$3 \times 9 = \boxed{}$
$9 \times 3 = \boxed{}$

Tips from teachers

Use the facts your child may already know (such as 1×3, 2×3, 5×3 and 10×3) to help recall the others. For example, 3×4 is double 3×2, 3×6 is 3 more than 3×5 and 3×9 is 3 less than 3×10. It is useful to point out that all the digits in all multiples of 3 have a sum of 3, 6 or 9, for example, $3 \times 9 = 27$ and $2 + 7 = 9$.

Colour the star when you complete the page.

7 Answer these.

3 × 1 = ☐

3 × 2 = ☐

3 × 3 = ☐

3 × 4 = ☐

3 × 5 = ☐

3 × 6 = ☐

3 × 7 = ☐

3 × 8 = ☐

3 × 9 = ☐

3 × 10 = ☐

3 × 11 = ☐

3 × 12 = ☐

Draw a line to match each multiplication with its array.
Look at them for 5 minutes and remember as many as you can.

Have a go

8 Circle the numbers that are in the 3 times table.

1 2 3 4 5 6 7 8 9 10 11 12 13 14 15

16 17 18 19 20 21 22 23 24 25 26 27 28 29 30

23

Multiplying by 4

I'll tell you something special – the numbers in the 4 times table are double the 2 times table and they are always even numbers. Take a look at these.

$2 \times 3 = 6 \rightarrow$ double $\rightarrow 4 \times 3 = 12$

Get ready

1. Colour the even numbers.

2. Circle the numbers that are in the 4 times table.

1	2	3	④	5	6	7	⑧	9	10	11	12	13	14	15	16	17	18	19	20
21	22	23	24	25	26	27	28	29	30	31	32	33	34	35	36	37	38	39	40

Write the next two numbers in each sequence. Use the number track to help you.

3. 4, 8, 12, ☐, ☐

4. 12, 16, 20, ☐, ☐

5. 24, 28, 32, ☐, ☐

6. 16, 20, 24, ☐, ☐

Tips from teachers

Your child should be able to recall the numbers in the 4 times table once they have a good knowledge of the 2 times table and can double numbers. Reinforce the fact that multiples of 4 are always even numbers.

7 Answer these.

4 × 1 = ☐

4 × 2 = ☐

4 × 3 = ☐

4 × 4 = ☐

4 × 5 = ☐

4 × 6 = ☐

4 × 7 = ☐

4 × 8 = ☐

4 × 9 = ☐

4 × 10 = ☐

4 × 11 = ☐

4 × 12 = ☐

Draw a line to match each multiplication with its array.

Have a go

1	2	3	4	5	6	7	8	9	10	11	12	13	14	15	16	17	18	19	20
21	22	23	24	25	26	27	28	29	30	31	32	33	34	35	36	37	38	39	40

Use the number line to answer these.

8 2 × 5 = ☐   **10** 2 × 10 = ☐   **12** 2 × 9 = ☐

   4 × 5 = ☐   4 × 10 = ☐   4 × 9 = ☐

9 2 × 3 = ☐   **11** 2 × 6 = ☐   **13** 2 × 8 = ☐

   4 × 3 = ☐   4 × 6 = ☐   4 × 8 = ☐

25

Colour the star when you complete the page.

Multiplication and division

Did you know that multiplication and division are linked? Take a look at these.

2 multiplied by 3 is 6.
2 × 3 = 6

6 divided by 2 is 3.
6 ÷ 2 = 3

Get ready

Answer these.

1

3 × 4 = ☐

12 ÷ 3 = ☐

3

2 × 6 = ☐

12 ÷ 2 = ☐

2

2 × 5 = ☐

10 ÷ 2 = ☐

4

5 × 3 = ☐

15 ÷ 5 = ☐

Tips from teachers

Understanding the inverse relationship between multiplication and division will help your child recall multiplication and division facts. Give trios of numbers such as 3, 5 and 15 and ask for the four related multiplication and division facts.

Colour the star when you complete the page.

⭐ Let's practise

Complete the facts for each number trio.

5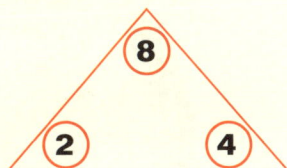

$2 \times \boxed{} = 8$

$4 \times \boxed{} = 8$

$8 \div 2 = \boxed{}$

$8 \div 4 = \boxed{}$

7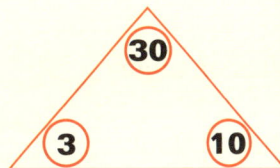

$3 \times \boxed{} = \boxed{}$

$10 \times \boxed{} = \boxed{}$

$30 \div \boxed{} = \boxed{}$

$30 \div \boxed{} = \boxed{}$

6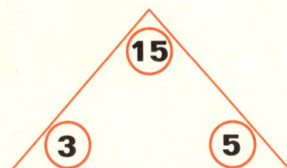

$3 \times \boxed{} = 15$

$5 \times \boxed{} = 15$

$15 \div 3 = \boxed{}$

$15 \div 5 = \boxed{}$

8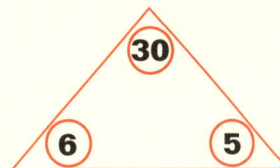

$6 \times \boxed{} = \boxed{}$

$5 \times \boxed{} = \boxed{}$

$30 \div \boxed{} = \boxed{}$

$30 \div \boxed{} = \boxed{}$

⭐ Have a go

Draw a picture to show $3 \times 4 = 12$ and $12 \div 3 = 4$.

Multiplication and division problems

I like baking at Kids Club. This recipe makes one cake.

4 spoonfuls of sugar

5 spoonfuls of flour

2 eggs

3 spoonfuls of butter

Get ready

Use the recipe card to work out the ingredients you need to make more cakes.

1 How much do you need to make 2 cakes?

☐ spoonfuls of sugar

☐ spoonfuls of flour

☐ eggs

☐ spoonfuls of butter

2 How much do you need to make 5 cakes?

☐ spoonfuls of sugar

☐ spoonfuls of flour

☐ eggs

☐ spoonfuls of butter

Tips from teachers

Encourage your child to draw pictures to represent each problem or use any pictures given to help multiply or divide. This will help them to understand the problem.

Colour the star when you complete the page.

3 There are 18 oranges. They are given to a group of children so each child has 3 oranges. How many children are in the group? ☐

4 15 trees are planted in a field. There are 5 rows and each row has the same number of trees. How many trees are in each row? ☐

5 A farmer has 40 eggs. She wants to put them in boxes which each hold 10 eggs. How many boxes will she need? ☐

6 A baker makes 20 cakes. He wants to put them in boxes which each hold 2 cakes. How many boxes does he need? ☐

Have a go

7 A chair has 4 legs and a stool has 3 legs.

There are 3 chairs and some stools in a room.

There are 18 legs altogether. How many stools are there? ☐

Number	Chair legs	Stool legs
1	4	3
2	8	
3	12	

How have I done?

Answer these questions to see how well you have done at Kids Club.

If the question is in two or more parts, you must get all the parts right to get a mark.

1

[ ] groups of 3 = [ ]

2

2 + 2 + 2 + 2 + 2 = [ ]

3 4 + 4 + 4 + 4 + 4 + 4 = [ ]

$4 \times 6 =$ [ ]

4 10 + 10 + 10 + 10 + 10 = [ ]

$10 \times 5 =$ [ ]

5 Complete these.

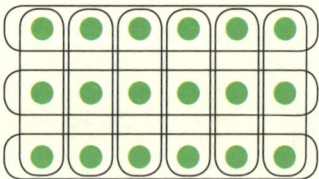

a) $3 \times$ [ ] = [ ]

b) $6 \times$ [ ] = [ ]

6 What is double 4? [ ]

Colour the star when you complete the page.

7 What is double 7? ☐

8 What number is half of 6? ☐

9 What number is half of 20? ☐

10 9 divided by 3 is ☐

11 20 divided by 5 is ☐

12 Circle **two** multiplications that make **12**.

3 × 6   7 × 2   3 × 5   4 × 3   5 × 2   2 × 6

13 0 × 9 = ☐

14 8 × 1 = ☐

15 3 × 7 = ☐

7 × 3 = ☐

16 Write the next two numbers in the 3 times table.

3   6   9   12   ☐   ☐

17 4 × 6 = ☐

6 × 4 = ☐

18 Circle the numbers in the 4 times table.

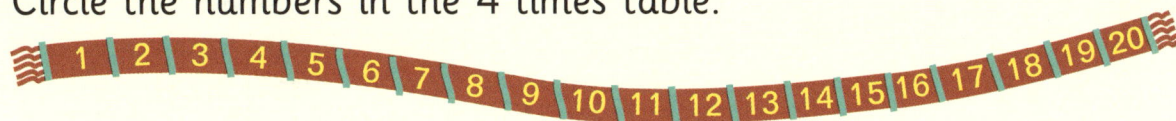

19

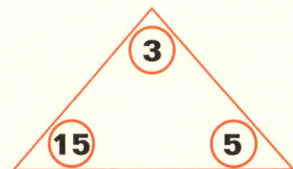

3 × ☐ = ☐   15 ÷ 3 = ☐

5 × ☐ = ☐   15 ÷ 5 = ☐

20 There are 14 socks on a washing line. When the socks are dry they are put in groups of 2 to make pairs. How many pairs of socks are there? ☐

Colour the star when you complete the page.

Answers

Pages 6–7
1 2, 6
2 4, 20
3 2, 20
4 4, 8
5 4, 16
6 3, 15
7 4, 12
8 2, 4
9 5, 20
10 5, 15
11 2, 10
12 4, 6
13 3, 8
14 2, 12
15 24

Pages 8–9
1 9
2 12
3 15
4 8
5 20
6 21
7 8
8 20
9 10
10 15
11 28
12 30
13 4
14 16
15 16
16 18
17 20

Pages 10–11
1 10
2 6
3 40
4 30
5 16
6 18
7 20, 20
8 10, 10
9 30, 30
10 14, 14
11 9, 9
12 40, 40
13 2, 4, 6, 8, 10, 12, 14, 16, 18, 20

Pages 12–13
1 $2 \times 5 = 10$
2 $10 \times 3 = 30$
3 $3 \times 6 = 18$
4 $5 \times 5 = 25$
5 $5 \times 8 = 40$
6 $2 \times 6 = 12$
7 $3 \times 5 = 15$
8 $2 \times 4 = 8$
9 $10 \times 3 = 30$
10 $2 \times 9 = 18$
11 $2 \times 6 = 12$, $6 \times 2 = 12$
12 $2 \times 8 = 16$, $8 \times 2 = 16$
13 $3 \times 5 = 15$, $5 \times 3 = 15$

Pages 14–15
1 10
2 6
3 8
4 12
5 1, 2, 3, 4, 5, 6
6 $16 \div 2 \rightarrow 8$
$8 \times 2 \rightarrow 16$
$12 \div 2 \rightarrow 6$
$9 \times 2 \rightarrow 18$
$20 \div 2 \rightarrow 10$
$3 \times 2 \rightarrow 6$
$40 \div 2 \rightarrow 20$
$6 \times 2 \rightarrow 12$
$10 \times 2 \rightarrow 20$
$7 \times 2 \rightarrow 14$

Pages 16–17
1 8
2 8
3 7
4 6
5 8 grouped into 2 = 4 groups
8 divided by 2 = 4
6 15 grouped into 5 = 3 groups
15 divided by 5 = 3
7 12 grouped into 4 = 3 groups

12 divided by 4 = 3
8 6 grouped into 3 = 2 groups
6 divided by 3 = 2
9 10 grouped into 5 = 2 groups
10 divided by 5 = 2
10 12 grouped into 3 = 4 groups
12 divided by 3 = 4
11 12
12 8
13 6
14 4

Pages 18–19
1–3

4 2, 4, 6, 8, 10, 12, 14, 16, 18, 20, 22, 24
5, 10, 15, 20, 25, 30, 35, 40, 45, 50, 55, 60
10, 20, 30, 40, 50, 60, 70, 80, 90, 100, 110, 120
5 $10 \times 1 \rightarrow 10$
$5 \times 2 \rightarrow 10$
$2 \times 6 \rightarrow 12$
$5 \times 3 \rightarrow 15$
$2 \times 9 \rightarrow 18$
$2 \times 10 \rightarrow 20$
$5 \times 4 \rightarrow 20$
$5 \times 5 \rightarrow 25$
$5 \times 6 \rightarrow 30$
$10 \times 3 \rightarrow 30$
$10 \times 4 \rightarrow 40$
$5 \times 8 \rightarrow 40$
$5 \times 9 \rightarrow 45$
$5 \times 10 \rightarrow 50$

Pages 20–21
1 1×6 and 6×1
2 8×0 and 0×8
3 4×1 and 1×4
4 0×5 and 5×0
5 1×9 and 9×1
6 7×0 and 0×7
7 circled $\rightarrow 5 \times 0$, 3×0, 6×0, 4×0, 9×0, 0×2, 0×8, 0×1, 0×7, $2 \times 1 \rightarrow 2$, $1 \times 3 \rightarrow 3$, $8 \times 1 \rightarrow 8$, $5 \times 1 \rightarrow 5$, $1 \times 9 \rightarrow 9$, $6 \times 1 \rightarrow 6$, $1 \times 7 \rightarrow 7$
8 8
9 0
10 0
11 4
12 6
13 0
14 0
15 9

Pages 22–23
1 6, 6
2 15, 15
3 30, 30
4 21, 21
5 18, 18
6 27, 27
7 3, 6, 9, 12, 15, 18, 21, 24, 27, 30, 33, 36
Check the correct array is joined to each multiplication.
8 3, 6, 9, 12, 15, 18, 21, 24, 27, 30

Pages 24–25
1 2, 4, 6, 8, 10, 12, 14, 16, 18, 20, 22, 24, 26, 28, 30, 32, 34, 36, 38, 40
2 4, 8, 12, 16, 20, 24, 28, 32, 36, 40
3 16, 20
4 24, 28
5 36, 40
6 28, 32
7 4, 8, 12, 16, 20, 24, 28, 32, 36, 40, 44, 48
Check the correct array is joined to each multiplication.
8 10, 20
9 6, 12
10 20, 40
11 12, 24
12 18, 36
13 16, 32

Pages 26–27
1 12, 4
2 10, 5
3 12, 6
4 15, 3
5 4, 2, 4, 2
6 5, 3, 5, 3
7 $3 \times 10 = 30$, $10 \times 3 = 30$, $30 \div 10 = 3$, $30 \div 3 = 10$
8 $6 \times 5 = 30$, $5 \times 6 = 30$, $30 \div 5 = 6$, $30 \div 6 = 5$
Ask how the drawing shows $3 \times 4 = 12$ and $12 \div 3 = 4$.

Pages 28–29
1 8 spoonfuls of sugar
10 spoonfuls of flour
4 eggs
6 spoonfuls of butter
2 20 spoonfuls of sugar
25 spoonfuls of flour
10 eggs
15 spoonfuls of butter
3 6 children
4 3 trees
5 4 egg boxes
6 10 boxes
7 2 stools

How have I done?
(Pages 30–31)
1 4, 12
2 10
3 24, 24
4 50, 50
5 a) 6, 18
b) 3, 18
6 8
7 14
8 3
9 10
10 3
11 4
12 4×3, 2×6
13 0
14 8
15 21, 21
16 15, 18
17 24, 24
18 4, 8, 12, 16, 20
19 $3 \times 5 = 15$ $15 \div 3 = 5$
$5 \times 3 = 15$ $15 \div 5 = 3$
20 7 pairs